Ivanhoe Masonic Quartettes

Also from Westphalia Press

westphaliapress.org

The Idea of the Digital University

Masonic Tombstones and Masonic Secrets

Treasures of London

The History of Photography

L'Enfant and the Freemasons

Baronial Bedrooms

Making Trouble for Muslims

Material History and Ritual Objects

Paddle Your Own Canoe

Opportunity and Horatio Alger

Careers in the Face of Challenge

Bookplates of the Kings

Collecting American Presidential Autographs

Freemasonry in Old Buffalo

Original Cables from the Pearl Harbor Attack

Social Satire and the Modern Novel

The Essence of Harvard

The Genius of Freemasonry

A Definitive Commentary on Bookplates

James Martineau and Rebuilding Theology

No Bird Lacks Feathers

Earthworms, Horses, and Living Things

The Man Who Killed President Garfield

Anti-Masonry and the Murder of Morgan

Understanding Art

Homeopathy

Ancient Masonic Mysteries

Collecting Old Books

Masonic Secret Signs and Passwords

The Thomas Starr King Dispute

Earl Warren's Masonic Lodge

Lariats and Lassos

Mr. Garfield of Ohio

The Wisdom of Thomas Starr King

The French Foreign Legion

War in Syria

Naturism Comes to the United States

New Sources on Women and Freemasonry

Designing, Adapting, Strategizing in Online Education

Gunboat and Gun-runner

Meeting Minutes of Naval Lodge No. 4 F.A.A.M

Ivanhoe Masonic Quartettes

Selected and Arranged by Thomas C. Pollack

with a new introduction by Sion Honea

WESTPHALIA PRESS
An imprint of Policy Studies Organization

Ivanhoe Masonic Quartettes

Westphalia Press
An imprint of Policy Studies Organization
1527 New Hampshire Ave., NW
Washington, D.C. 20036
dgutierrezs@ipsonet.org

ISBN-13: 978-1935907466
ISBN-10: 1935907468

Updated material and comments on this edition
can be found at the Westphalia Press website:
www.westphaliapress.org

Nineteenth-Century American Masonic Songbooks: A Preliminary Checklist

... the tie of common membership, flat and without content as it is, bolstered up by sentimental songs which no one really likes to sing but which everyone would miss if they weren't sung, has an intensity of its own.

Margaret Mead[1]

DURING THE NINETEENTH CENTURY, FRATERNAL ORGANIZATIONS IN the United States achieved a popularity as social institutions surpassed only by organized religion. In some urban centers the number of fraternal lodges even surpassed the number of churches by two and three times.[2] From a modest beginning estimated at 3,000 members in 1800, fraternal organizations are estimated to have included 6,000,000 members in hundreds of organizations by the end of the century.[3] By 1925, just before their dramatic decline, there were over 800 distinct orders with members numbering perhaps as many as 35,000,000.[4] This prodigious activity must necessarily indicate something about American society and its workings, despite the fact that fraternal orders have "usually been dismissed as the harmless addiction of a somewhat addled 'nation of joiners'—altogether too trivial for serious explanation."[5] This attitude is unfortunate, for the social orders provide convenient and representative microcosms for the analysis of the larger society in which they existed. Lynn Dumenil, speaking specifically of Freemasonry, noted it "mirrored middle-class values," and it offered its members a means of identifying the values of the middle-class world of the nineteenth century.[6] Within the last decade, however, professional scholars have begun to redress this neglect, producing excellent works in widely diverging areas of the field.[7]

This general neglect being the rule until recently, it is not surprising that research has also overlooked the music associated with these orders, music that they used for their rituals and lodge functions, their education, and their entertainment. Yet, a signicant amount of material for its study does exist, albeit in a nearly completely disorganized condition. Even a brief survey of the material reveals that the preponderant amount of it is specifically associated with the fraternal order of Free and Accepted Masons.

It is natural that the Freemasons should predominate, for they were the oldest, the most prestigious, and the archetype on which the other orders patterned themselves. Growing apparently out of the operative lodges of medieval stonemasons, the order organized itself officially in London in 1717. From there it spread rapidly throughout the English speaking world and, in various forms, into western Europe by the end of the eighteenth century. Its forms of initiation, ritualistic style, organizational structure, symbolism, peculiarities in language, and other features were imitated again and again in the nineteenth century by hundreds of social, vocational, and academic fraternal orders. As such, its value as the "type" of fraternal orders is unrivaled, while it also provides an easily definable subfield for investigation.

On the face of the evidence itself, music was an important part of Masonic life at least as early as the mid-eighteenth century, by which time it had stimulated the production of songbooks directed exclusively to Masonic audiences.[8] The music itself can be divided into three broad, overlapping categories: functional music for lodge rituals, music of edifying nature explicitly or implicitly Masonic in sentiment, and non-Masonic music of a social or entertaining nature. Functional music was intended to accompany or illustrate the variety of ritualistic or formal activities of the lodge. Somewhat different is the large amount of music of a serious and edifying nature that was not intended to accompany the rituals, but tended to extol Masonic ideals and virtues.[9] The innumerable parties, banquets, festivals, and drinking bouts of the fraternity called for accompaniment by another type of convivial music, sometimes reflecting its specifically Masonic context. The latter two categories of non-ritualistic music seem designed for the broader purpose of providing entertainment or filling the needs of the lodge singing club.

The repertoire itself is drawn from an extremely wide range of sources: classical art, music, traditional tunes, hymns, drinking songs, popular songs of the day, light choral music, and instrumental works. It consists mainly of part songs, typically for three voices of the glee type, but also includes a wide variety of solo songs, duets, rounds, catches, and instrumental pieces. This repertoire provides an index to the actual musical life of middle-class America in the nineteenth century. As such it offers the researcher a large number of intriguing questions. What are the exact components of the repertoire? What do they say about society at the time? Who were the composers that reached into this substratum of middle-class life? What was the repertoire of traditional tunes utilized? What were the hymn tunes? What was the relative influence of secular versus sacred sources? How did the repertoire change over time and how did it remain the same? Are there indications of social change in the changes detectable in the collections and their contents? What conclusions can be drawn concerning the penetration of classical music into the popular realm? What types of ensembles were typical? What were the musical resources commonly available? What do the printing and publishing practices indicate about the dissemination of the music in relation to the larger music market of the time? The list might well continue almost indefinitely.

As it stands, however, there is no way of answering these questions, for the repertoire is as inaccessible as could well be possible in this day. The collections of music libraries usually neglect the songbooks—another result of the "too trivial for serious explanation" attitude. When such materials can be found in collections, they are usually few in number and insufficiently identified. Those collections that do possess them in quantity—fraternal libraries, such as the Livingston Masonic Library—tend also to neglect the material as being musical and so out of the ordinary realm of bibliographic control. If the materials are cataloged at all, it is usually superficially done. These fraternal libraries are also not well integrated into the world of networking, and so their collections tend to be accessible only on site and with great difficulty, often not through a catalog but through an individual.

The difficulty of obtaining the pertinent material is paralleled by difficulties in defining and delimiting it. For this reason, virtually every descriptive term utilized in the title of this essay requires further definition. The chronological boundaries are ostensibly 1800–1899, yet in practice I have included a few earlier imprints on the somewhat arbitrary grounds of intrinsic interest, or for the purpose of historical continuity. I have, however, made no deliberate effort to include eighteenth century imprints. Irving Lowens' work provides an excellent access to those works.[10]

The term "American" also requires definition as it presents both geographical and conceptual difficulties. It has so happened that I have discovered no imprints issued outside the confines of the continental United States. A variety of factors possibly help to explain this. Freemasonry was largely an English-speaking phenomenon and so, with some exceptions, alien to Latin American countries until this century. One might speculate that the Canadian "market," on the other hand, would have been dominated by publications from the United States and England, thereby inhibiting domestic production. The perceived ephemeral nature of the material is also a major factor influencing its survival and our knowledge of it. It should be noted as well that the selection procedure employed here is indiscriminate as to language. Both German and French language American imprints have so far come to light.

The question of foreign language American imprints leads naturally to the issue of the widespread use of foreign publications, particularly English ones, in American countries. This was unquestionably a widespread practice as shown by the reissue of English works in American editions. Under the year 1782 Lowens lists Laurence Dermott's *Ahiman Rezon*, which he concludes is not an American imprint but circulated widely in America. In 1783 Hall and Sellers of Philadelphia issued the first of many reprints and reworkings (Lowens 34).[11] Also according to Lowens, the first songster printed in this country was Benjamin Franklin's edition of the English Grand Lodge's *Constitutions* of James Anderson.[12] The repertoire itself also yields unmistakable evidence of English or British Isles origin in the occasional citation of lodge names, performers, performance sites, and authors clearly originating in the United Kingdom. I have chosen to exclude all but actual American imprints. While I readily acknowledge that the English origin of the repertoire is contextually important for its study, my intention here is the more narrow one of determining the specifically American activity in this field.

The term *Masonic* as used here includes all organizations claiming Masonic antecedents. This includes not only the traditional craft lodges and their officially recognized concordant bodies of the so-called Scottish and York Rites, but also all bodies speciffically claiming a Masonic character or origin whether or not officially "recognized" by the "established" bodies. In practice this has presented no problem, for I have yet to discover any works issuing from or intended for use by any other than the traditional established bodies.

My definition of songbooks is considerably narrower than Lowens' definition of songster.[13] I use the term songbook to include published works whose main, or at least a main, purpose is to provide a collection of secular materials for singing, with or without music. Of course, in application no such definition is so neat. A good example is *The True Ahiman Rezon*, a book whose main purpose is to provide a kind of miscellaneous companion to and manual for the practice of Freemasonry, but which includes a large, discrete collection of songs that it would be imprudent to omit. It would, in fact, be easier to describe the type of materials that I have systematically excluded. These embrace mainly lodge monitors, manuals, handbooks, companions, etc., that contain, interspersed within their contents, a few songs for specific purposes. Although such works are important for reconstructing the use of music in the formal lodge context, their importance for reconstructing the repertoire is miniscule, for most simply draw upon selections from that repertoire.

A word should even be said about "preliminary." So complex, confusing, and chaotically disorganized were the publishing practices of those issuing the songbooks, and the remains of them so desultory and inaccessible that it may well be that all bibliographic research into them is fated to the status of "preliminary." It appears that some items were printed in small quantities, almost "on demand," each issue being fitted out with such illustrations, frontispiece, notices, advertisements, etc., as were on hand at the time. For instance, almost every copy of Luke Eastman's *Masonick Melodies* that I have yet seen varies to some degree in those respects, but not at all in repertoire. Almost every "edition" of *The Masonic Harp* bears a different title page proclaiming a distinct edition by a distinct publisher, while the musical contents are indistinguishable. This seems typical of the practice later in the century, when publishers were purchased, publishing rights or type sold, and works issued in multiple "editions" almost annually with no detectable difference except title page, date, edition number or publisher's advertisements. This state of affairs would actually make an interesting study in the practices of music printing and publishing of popular music of a social and entertaining nature, but it has little effect on the nature of the repertoire itself.

Nonetheless, the intent of this essay is to make a beginning on giving access to this potentially intriguing and important repertoire. I hope that it may stimulate both communication concerning the existence and nature of materials and also research into the issues of the music and the manner of its publication.

I have examined a majority, but not all, of the items listed. For those examined, I provide very brief notes on their nature, mainly the presence of music and indexes. I have also provided the OCLC (Online Computer Library Catalog) number of each item for which one could be found. An asterisk applied to the OCLC number indicates that records for other editions exist. Since the main purpose here is to give access to the repertoire, I have cited different editions of the same work only when they are distinctive in repertoire. however slight. In so doing, I have cited the earliest edition that could be identified. In the infrequent instances where I have not been able to examine the oldest edition, I have cited both the oldest identified and the one that I did examine.[14]

I use the following abbreviations:

HT House of the Temple, Library of the Supreme Council, Southern Jurisdiction, Ancient and Accepted Scottish Rite, Washington D.C.

LML Livingston Masonic Library, Grand Lodge of New York, Free and Accepted Masons, New York City.

Lowens Irving Lowens. *A Bibliography of Songsters Printed in America Before 1821.* Worcester: American Antiquarian Society, 1976.

THE BIBLIOGRAPHY

Allgemeines maurerisches liederbuch zum gebrauch der logen fr. und ang. maurer. Ed. Röhr. Williamsburg, Long Island: Triangeld, [1856].
58 pp. 14 cm.
Texts only, tunes indicated, index: first lines.
LML

The Apollo: being a collection of English songs, including a selection of masonic songs, anthems, odes, preludes, prologues, epilogues, toasts, etc. Philadelphia. W. Spotswood, 1791.
164 p. 15 cm.
Not examined.
*OCLC: 20321624, Lowens 58

The Apollo: being a collection of English songs, including a selection of masonic songs, anthems, odes, preludes, prologues, epilogues, toasts, etc. A new edition with additions. Philadelphia: W. Spotswood, 1793.
164 p. 16 cm.
Texts only, tunes occasionally indicated, index: first lines.
*OCLC: 4950636, Lowens 71, HT

Barrett's collection of sacred music for men's voices, for masonic and church use. Ed. Francis J. Barrett. New York: Molineux, n.d.
56 p. 27 cm.
Texts with music, tune indicated, no index.
LML

The Columbian songster and freemason's pocket companion. A collection of the newest and most celebrated sentimental, convivial, humourous, satirical, pastoral, hunting, sea and masonic songs, being the largest and best collection ever published in America. Ed. S. Larkin. Portsmouth, N.H.: J. Melcher, 1798.
x, 216 p. 18 cm.
Texts only, tunes occasionally indicated, index: title.
OCLC: 21913869, Lowens 145, HT

The Conclave musical manual. Ed. James B. Taylor. n.p.: n.p., 1877.
[16] p. 22 cm.
Texts only, tunes indicated, no index.
HT, LML

XXVIII. SONG.

To the Tune of *Jerry Fitzgerald.*

I.

King *Solomon*, that wife Projecture,
In Mafonry took great Delight;
And *Hiram*, that great Architecture,
Whofe Actions fhall ever fhine bright:
From the Heart of a true honeft Mafon,
There's none can the Secret remove;
Our Maxims are Juftice, Morality,
Friendfhip, and brotherly Love.
Fa, la, la, *&c.*

II.

We meet like true Friends on the Square,
And part on a Level that's fair;
Alike we refpect King and Beggar,
Provided they're juft and fincere:
We fcorn an ungenerous Action,
None can with Free-Mafons compare;
We love for to live within Compafs,
By Rules that are honeft and fair.
Fa, la, la, *&c.*

III.

Succefs to all Accepted Mafons,
Their's none can their Honour pull down;
Fore'er fince the glorious Creation,
Thefe brave Men were held in Renown:

When

"Song XXVIII," from Laurence Dermott, *Ahiman Rezon: or A Help to a Brother; shewing the Excellency of Secrecy, and the first Cause, or Motive, of the Institution of Free-Masonry* (London: 1756; reprint, Bloomington, Ill.: Masonic Book Club, 1975), pp. 132,133.

When *Adam* was King of all Nations,
He form'd a Plan with all Speed;
And ſoon made a ſweet Habitation,
For him and his Companion *Eve*.
Fa, la, la, *&c*.

IV.

We exclude all talkative Fellows,
That will babble and prate paſt their Wit;
They ne'er ſhall come into our Secret,
For they're neither worthy nor fit:
But the Perſons that's well recommended,
And we find them honeſt and true;
When our Lodge is well tyl'd we'll prepare 'em,
And like Maſons our Work we'll purſue.
Fa, la, la, *&c*.

V.

There's ſome fooliſh People reject us,
For which they're highly to blame;
They cannot ſhew any Objection,
Or Reaſon for doing the ſame:
The Art's a divine Inſpiration,
As all honeſt Men will declare;
So here's to all true-hearted Brothers,
That live within Compaſs and Square.
Fa, la, la, *&c*.

To all thoſe who live within Compaſs and Square.

XXIX. Song

[Dermott, Laurence.] ***Ahiman rezon abridged and digested: as a help to all that are, or would be Free and Accepted Masons.*** Philadelphia: Hall and Sellers, 1783.
xvi, 166 p.
pp. 115144: a collection of Masons songs.
Not examined. Lowens 34.

Dermott, Laurence. *The True ahiman rezon: or a help to all that are, or would be free and accepted masons.* With many additions. The first American from the third London edition. New York: Southwick & Harcdastle [sic]: 1805. 216, 60 p. 18 cm. A separate title pages appears on p. 131. A Collection of masonic songs with several ingenious prologues and epilogues to which is added Solomon's Temple, an oratorio, as it was performed for the benefit of sick and distressed free-masons. New York: Southwick & Hardcastle, n.d.
131211 p.
Texts only, tunes occasionally indicated, no index.
*OCLC: 12003412

The Free-mason's companion. Being a choice collection of the newest and most celebrated masonic songs. New York: John Tiebout, 1802.
40 p.
Not examined.
Lowens 230

The Freemason's hymnal, a collection of original and selected hymns, odes and songs for the use of lodges, chapters and commanderies. Ed. W. Malmene. St. Louis: Southwestern Book & Publishing Co., 1871.
vi, 72 p. 15 cm.
Texts only, tunes indicated, index: subject, first line.
*OCLC: 6856170 [record states 1871 = 2nd ed., not verifiable this copy], HT

The Free-mason's vocal assistant and register of the lodges of masons in South Carolina and Georgia. Charleston: J.J. Negrin, 1807.
255 p. 18 cm.
Texts only, tunes occasionally indicated, index: title.
OCLC: 6912124, Lowens 336, HT

The Gems of masonry; emblematic and descriptive. Ed. John Sherer. Cincinnati: John Sherer, 1859.
iii, 52 p. 19 cm.
Texts only, tunes occasionally indicated, no index.
OCLC: 4442625, HT

Holden's sacred music for men's voices, for masonic and church use. Ed. Albert J. Holden.Boston: Oliver Ditson, 1893.
128 p. 25 cm.
Texts with music, tunes occasionally indicated, index: title.
*OCLC: 18940069, LML

Ivanhoe masonic quartettes. New York: Wm. A. Pond, 1867.
[iv], 75 p. 25 cm.
Texts with music, tunes rarely indicated, index: subject.
OCLC: 8798458, HT, LML

"Master Mason" to the familiar tune of Pleye's Hymn, from Henry Stephen Cutler, *The Masonic harmonia; a collection of music, original and selected, for the use of the masonic fraternity* (New York: Masonic Publishing and Manufacturing Co., 1871), p. 65.

Liederbuch der ger. u. vollk. St. Johannis-Loge Pythagoras i.D.v. New York. New York: Associations Buchdruckerei, 1850.
136 p. 17 cm.
Texts only, no tunes indicated, no index.
HT, LML

Liederbuch der ger. und vollk. Schiller-Loge, No. 304, i.D.v. Williamsburg. L.I., New York: Teubner, 1854.
29 p. 18 cm.
Not examined.
HT

Lodge Music! A selection of familiar odes set to familiar tunes, arranged within the compass of all voices. Ed. George F. Ilsley. New York: Macoy, 1897.
14 p. 19 cm.
Texts with music, no tunes indicated, no index.
OCLC: 20598967, HT

The Manual of masonic music. In two parts: I. containing music for masonic ceremonies, and the masonic social circle. II. containing masonic odes, songs, anthems, etc. Ed. James B. Taylor. New York: Jno. W. Leonard & Co. American Masonic Agency, 1856.
336 p. 23 cm.
This work was printed as volume 24 of Universal Masonic Library, cf. OCLC 13024961
Texts with music, some texts alone with tune indicated, index: odes with music.
LML

The Masonic choir: a collection of hymns and tunes, original and selected, for the use of the fraternity. Ed. John W. Dadmun; arr. O.B. Brown. Boston: G.D. Russell & Co., 1864.
96 p. 20 cm.
Texts with music, tunes occasionally indicated, index: subject, tune.
*OCLC: 24824276, LML

The Masonic choralist. A collection of odes, chants, marches, and other musical services for the use of the blue lodge. Ed. Harvey C. Camp. New York: H.C. Camp, 1878.
48 pp.
Texts with music, tunes indicated, index: subject.
HT, LML

The Masonic concordia. A collection of odes for the various ceremonies and festivals of the masonic fraternity. Ed. George F. Ilsley. New York: D.B. Howell & Co., 1872.
54 p. 15 cm.
Text only, tunes indicated by cross-reference to Mystic Chord, no index.
*OCLC: 6859397 [= 1876 ed.], LML

The Masonic harmonia; a collection of music, original and selected, for the use of the masonic fraternity. Ed. Henry Stephen Cutler. New York: Masonic Publishing & Mfg. Co., 1867.
120 p. 18 cm.
Texts with music, tunes not indicated, no index.
OCLC: 14164223, HT, LML

N

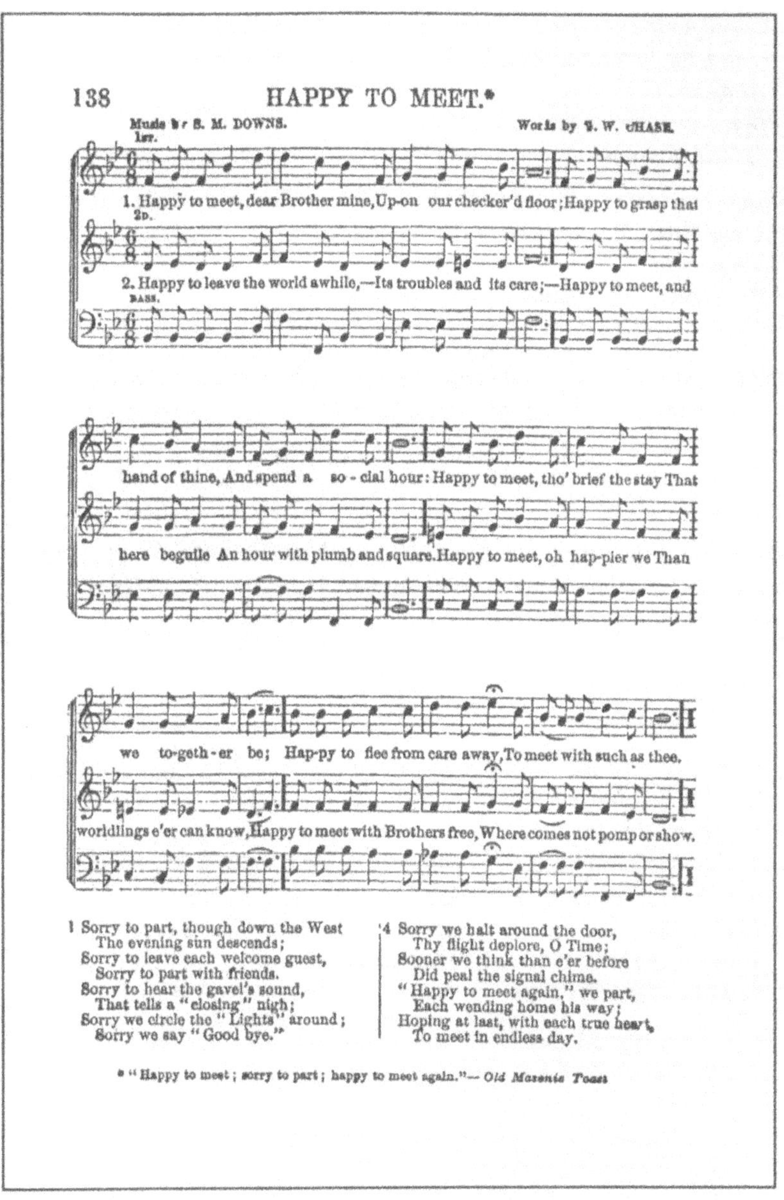

138 HAPPY TO MEET.*

Music by S. M. DOWNS. Words by G. W. CHASE.

3 Sorry to part, though down the West
The evening sun descends;
Sorry to leave each welcome guest,
Sorry to part with friends.
Sorry to hear the gavel's sound,
That tells a "closing" nigh;
Sorry we circle the "Lights" around;
Sorry we say "Good bye."

4 Sorry we halt around the door,
Thy flight deplore, O Time;
Sooner we think than e'er before
Did peal the signal chime.
"Happy to meet again," we part,
Each wending home his way;
Hoping at last, with each true heart,
To meet in endless day.

* "Happy to meet; sorry to part; happy to meet again."—*Old Masonic Toast*

"Happy to Meet," from George Wingate Chase, *The Masonic Harp: A Collection of Masonic Odes, Hymns, Songs &c. for the public and private Ceremonies and Festivals of the Fraternity* (Boston: Oliver Ditson & Co., 1868), p. 138.

The Masonic harp: a collection of masonic odes, hymns, songs, etc. for the public and private ceremonies and festivals of the fraternity. Ed. George W. Chase. Boston: Oliver Ditson & Co., 1858.
ix, 160 p. 18 cm.
Texts with music, tunes indicated, index: subject, first line, tune.
*OCLC: 16706099, LML

The Masonic lyre; containing a collection of masonic odes, original and selected, intended for the use of lodges: to which is added, the chapter odes, now in general use; also, the funeral service. Ed. W.B. Rockwood. New York: James Narine, 1851.
44 pp. 20 cm.
Texts only, tunes indicated, no index.
OCLC: 21430406, HT

Masonic melodies: adapted to the ceremonies and festivals of the fraternity. Ed. Thomas Power. Boston: Oliver Ditson, 1844.
108 p. 24 cm.
Texts only, tunes indicated, index: subject, first line.
*OCLC: 16878806, HT, LML

The Masonic minstrel: containing select odes with music for the lodge, chapter and encampment. Ed. Robert Macoy. New York: Clark, Austin, & Smith, 1856.
64 p. 11 cm.
Texts most with music, no tunes indicated, no index.
HT, LML

The Masonic museum; or, freemason's companion. A collection of songs, choruses, odes, etc. adapted to the use of chapters and lodges. Ed. J. Hardcastle. New York: J. Hardcastle, 1816.
76 p. 17 cm.
Texts only, tunes rarely indicated, no index.
OCLC: 20768168, Lowens 517, HT, LML

The Masonic musical manual: being a selection of old recognized songs, odes, and anthems of the craft, with the original music, together with new songs, odes, and anthems, by standard masonic writers, appropriate to the several degrees and ceremonies as practised by the ancient craft masons. Ed. Henry Watson. New York: H. Watson, 1855.
80 p. 25 cm.
Texts only, no tunes indicated, index: subject.
OCLC: 20673334, HT, LML

The Masonic ode, a collection of solos, quartets, and choruses, adapted to the uses of the fraternity. Ed. Powell G. Fithian. Boston: Oliver person, 1890.
68 p. 19 cm.
Texts with music, tunes indicated, index: subject, first line, tunes, meters, chants.
OCLC: 20588499, HT, LML

"Hark the Hiram," from [David Vinton], *The Masonick Minstrel, a Selection of Masonick, Sentimental, and Humorous Songs, Duets, Glees, Canons, Rounds, and Canzonets Respectfully Dedicated to the Most Ancient and Honourable Fraternity of Free and Accepted Masons* (Denham, Mass.: Hermann Mann, 1816), p.141.

Masonic odes. Ancient City Lodge, No. 452, F.&A.M. Albany, N.Y. Ed. Frederick Lawrence. Albany: Van Beuthuysen, 1876.
50 p. 18 cm.
Texts only, no tunes indicated, no index.
HT, LML

Masonic odes: also the masonic funeral service intended for the use of Munn Lodge No. 190. of the ancient and honorable fraternity of free and accepted masons of the city of New York. New York: Taws, Russell & Co.: n.d.
30 p. 16 cm.
Texts only, tunes indicated, no index.
LML

The Masonic orpheus. A collection of songs, hymns, chants, and familiar tunes especially designed to accompany the work of free and accepted masons, in all the various degrees and orders appertaining to the blue lodge, chapter, council, and commandery; also adapted to all public and private ceremonies of the fraternity, installation, dedication, funeral obsequies, etc., arranged for male voices. Ed. Howard M. Dow. Boston: Oliver Ditson, 1870.
202 p. 25 x 35 cm.
Texts with music, tunes indicated, index: first line.
OCLC: 6338285, HT, LML

Masonic song book, containing a large collection of the most approved masonic songs, odes, anthems, etc. Philadelphia: M. Carey, 1814.
164, [3] p. 18 cm.
Texts only, tunes indicated, index: title.
OCLC: 20782253, Lowens 471, HT

Masonic Songs, containing a selection of music and words, for various occasions, as used by the ancient order of F.&A.M. Chicago: H. M. Higgins, 1862.
10 p. 13 x 21 cm.
Texts with music, no tunes indicated, no index.
HT

Masonic songs, oratorios, anthems, prologues, and toasts adapted to the different degrees of masonry. Waterford: James Lyon, 1797.
vii, 140 p. 12 cm.
Texts only, tunes rarely indicated, index: title.
Lowens 131, HT, LML

The Masonic vocal manual. Ed. Robert Macoy. New York: Clark, Austin & Smith, 1854.
72 p. 15 cm.
Texts only, tunes indicated, index: tide.
*OCLC: 20666779, LML

Masonic vocal manual. Ed. Robert Macoy. New York: Masonic Manufacturing Co., 1867.
48 p. 15 cm.
Texts only, tunes indicated, no index. This is essentially a reproduction of the 1854 edition without the title index. This edition was the source for numerous subsequent reprint editions.
LML

Masonick melodies, being a choice selection of the most approved masonick songs, duets, glees, catches, cannons [sic], hymns, odes, dirges, choruses, appropriate to all masonick occasions, the whole set to musick: and respectfully dedicated to the most ancient and honorable fraternity of free and accepted masons. Ed. Luke Eastman. Boston: T. Howe, 1818.
viii, 204, [4] p. 20 cm.
Texts with music, tunes occasionally indicated, index: title.
OCLC: 3394073, HT, LML

The Masonick minstrel. A selection of masonick, sentimental, and humorous songs, duets, glees, canons, rounds and canzonets respectfully dedicated to the most ancient and honourable fraternity of free and accepted masons. Ed. David Vinton. Dedham, Mass.: Herman Mann, 1816.
[viii], 463, [1] p. 21 cm.
Texts with music, no tunes indicated, index: title.
*OCLC: 24537612, Lowens 518, LML

Melodies for the craft or, songs for freemasons. Suitable for every occasion. Cincinnati: Ernst, 1852.
151, [3] p. 16 cm.
Texts with music, no tunes indicated, index: title.
OCLC: 9406033, HT, LML

Muse of masonry. Comprising a number of masonic songs, chiefly adapted to familiar tunes, with appropriate toasts and sentiments. Together with a number of prayers generally made use of at the opening of a lodge, and making of a mason. New York: John Tiebout, 1801.
[ii], 64 p. 23 cm.
Not examined.
OCLC: 15455020 [microform], Lowens 217

Music of the chapter for royal arch masons. Ed. John B. Marsh. New York: Ditson, 1869.
38 p. 22 cm.
Texts with music, tunes indicated, index: subject.
HT, LML

The Mystic chord. A collection of masonic odes and melodies for the ceremonies and festivals of the fraternity, to which is added a choice selection of miscellaneous music. Ed. Chester W. Mabie. New York: by the author, 1866.
112 p. 20 cm.
Texts with music, tunes indicated, index: subject, tune, first line. Numerous subsequent reprints are unaltered until during the twentieth century, when the indexes are removed from the back to the front of the volume.
*OCLC: 13056891, HT, LML

The New masonic musical manual. Containing odes, chants, male quartets, solos and marches, adapted to the ceremonies of the fraternity, also organ solos, social songs and male quartets, for refreshment and special occasions, selected from the works of the best masters. 1st edition. Ed. William H. Janes. Park Row, N.Y.: Macoy, 1898.
[vi], 96 p. 26 cm.
Texts with music, tunes indicated, index: subject.
*OCLC: 6937897, LML

S

Odes for the use of Masonic Lodges. New York: Van & Co., 1899.
40 p. 19 cm.
Texts with music, tunes indicated, index: tune, first line.
LML

Recueil de cantiques de la loge française l'aménité, no. 73. Séante a l'or. Philadelphie. Philadelphia: Chez Thomas et William Bradford.
[1801]. 55 p.
Not examined.
OCLC: 21325342, Lowens 219

The Royal arch melodia. A collection of music, original and selected, for the use of chapters and councils. Ed. Chester W. Mabie. New York: Howell and Mabie, 1868.
72 p. 20 cm.
Texts with music, tunes indicated, index: subject, first line, tunes.
OCLC: 20749680 [= 1884 ed.], LML

A Selection of masonic odes and hymns for the use of St. John's lodge, no. 1, F.&A.M., for the various ceremonies of a master mason's lodge. Newark: A. Stephen Holbrook, 1862.
39 p. 25 cm.
Texts only, tunes indicated, no index.

The Vocal companion and masonic register. In two parts: Part I. consisting of original and selected masonic songs, anthems, dirges, prologues, epilogues, toasts and sentiments, charges, prayers, funerals procession, etc. Part II. a concise account of the origin of masonry in America: with a list of the lodges in the six northern states. Boston: John M. Dunham, 1802.
viii, 180, v, 103, v p. 18 cm.
Texts only, tunes mostly indicated, index: title.
OCLC: 22225156, Lowens 239, HT

NOTES

1. Margaret Mead, And Keep Your Powder Dry: An Anthropologist Looks at America (New York: William Morrow, 1942), p. 37.

2. Arthur M. Schlesinger, The Rise of the City 18781898 (New York: Macmillan, 1933), p. 290.

3. Schlesinger, p. 289.

4. Roland Berthoff, An Unsettled People: Social Order and Disorder in American History (New York: Harper & Row, 1971), p. 447.

5. Berthoff, p. 270.

6. Lynn Dumenil, Freemasonry and American Culture 1880–1930 (Princeton: Princeton, 1984), p. xii.

7. Among the major works are the following: Christopher McIntosh, *The Rose Cross and the Age of Reason* (Leiden: E.J. Brill, 1992); Mark Carnes, *Secret Ritual and Manhood in Victorian America* (New Haven: Yale, 1989); Margaret Jacob, *Living the Enlightenment: Freemasonry and Politics in Eighteenth-Century Europe* (New York: Oxford, 1991); Lynn Dumenil, *Freemasonry and American Culture 1880–1930* (Princeton: Princeton, 1984).

8. A. Sharp, "Masonic Songs and Song Books of the Late xviii century," Ars Quatuor Coronatorum, vol. 65 (1952), pp. 9495.

9. Such an edifying strain appears relatively early in the history of Freemasonry and cannot be neatly identified with the influence of the temperance and religious movements later in the nineteenth century, as some scholars tend (e.g., Berthoff, p. 270). It is perhaps both the natural outgrowth of the fraternity's expressed high ideals and the evidence of a reaction against the frequent reality of a fraternity operating below those ideals. It is interesting, and amusing, to detect this tension in at least one early songbook when the editor advises his readers that he presents to them a work "free from vulgar and objectionable sentiments, and which contains nothing but what will harmonize with their Moral designs." (*Masonick Melodies*. Luke Eastman, ed.,1818).

10. Irving Lowens, *A Bibliography of Songsters Printed in America Before 1821* (Worcester, Mass.: American Antiquarian Society, 1976).

11. In fact, this book with the inexplicable title took on a life of its own in the United States, continuing in use long after it had been dropped, in 1813, from use in England. The Grand Lodges of several states adopted the name itself for their own constitutions, thereby confusing the issue still more. "Ahiman Rezon," *Coil's Masonic Encyclopedia* (New York: Macoy Publishing and Masonic Supply Co., 1961).

12. Lowens, p. xi.

13. Lowens, p. ixx.

14. I would particularly like to thank Mr. William Moore, Director of the Livingston Masonic Library for his extensive and courteous assistance in making the library's excellent collection of songbooks available to me. The assistance of Kimberly Sprow, library research assistant at the House of the Temple Library has also been invaluable. I am also grateful to Laura Snyder of Sibley Music Library for many helpful suggestions. All defects are, of course, solely my own responsibility.

Sion M. Honea, P∴M∴

U

Editor's Note. *The previous article originally appeared as "Nineteenth-Century American Masonic Songbooks: A Preliminary Checklist,"* Music Reference Services Quarterly, *vol. 3 (1995), no. 4, pp. 17–32, ©1995 by The Haworth Press, Inc., Binghamton, N.Y., All Rights Reserved, and then later appeared under the same title in* Heredom: The Transactions of the Scottish Rite Research Society, *vol 6, pp. 285–304, 1997. It is reprinted here with the permission of the author and both journals.*

Selected and arranged by

Thomas C. Pollock.

Presented to
Wm Lyon Dobbs,
Nov. 16 - 1907
By
Prof. Grubb.
age
94 -

TO

WOR. BRO. A. A. VALENTINE,

MASTER OF IVANHOE LODGE, NO. 610, F. & A. M.,

THIS WORK

IS RESPECTFULLY DEDICATED BY

The Author.

PREFACE.

THE recognized want of appropriate Music, for the use of the Masonic Fraternity, has induced the compiler to publish the present work, which has been truly one of love.

The Music herein contained, with two exceptions, has been written and arranged for male voices; and although the pieces have been classified in the Index, it will be observed that there is no necessity of adhering strictly to this arrangement, as much of the Music may be used in any part of the ceremonies of the Masonic Order. The two pieces for mixed voices, "From the North" and "Anniversary Ode," will be found very appropriate for festivals, &c., where the assistance of the "gentler sex" may be had. The chants will also be found very effective, when properly rendered, in the working of the Degrees.

The subscriber trusts that the general excellence of the material herein contained, will recommend it to all musicians in the Fraternity, and do something towards raising the standard of music which, in our Lodges, is much behind "the age." Nothing is more elevating and inspiring than good music.

The introduction of quartette singing will add much, very much, to the beautiful ceremonies of the Craft; and there is no reason why music of this character should not be enjoyed by every Lodge throughout the country.

With these few remarks the present volume is given to the public, in the hope that its contents will meet with approbation.

THOMAS C. POLLOCK.

NEW YORK, *Dec. 1st*, 1867.

NOTE.—In accompanying the Male Quartettes, the right hand part should be played an octave lower than written throughout.

INDEX.

OPENING LODGE.

Sweet as the Dew........MOSENTHAL.... 1
Meeting..................OTTO.......... 3
Brotherly Love..........KUCKEN....... 5
Eternal Source..........................10
Within Our Temple.......BRISTOW.......12
From East to West.....................11

ENTERED APPRENTICE.

Far from the World's.....REICHARDT....14
Spirit of Pewer...........MORGAN.......18
While Journeying On.....WATSON.......57
Integer Vitae............FLEMMING.....19

FELLOW CRAFT.

Initiation.................HATTON.......22
Welcome.................THOMAS.......20

MASTER MASON.

Initiation.................BERGE........25
Quartette.................BRISTOW.......28
Strange Darkness........SHERWIN......30
The Last Degree.........WATSON.......54
Hear My Prayer.........BASSFORD......52

CLOSING LODGE.

Sweet as the Dew........MUNGER.......31
Lo! the Day at Last.....FLOTOW.......34
Parting..................SHERWIN......40
Parting Ode.............MUNGER.......37

MISCELLANEOUS.

Installation.............MORGAN.......41
Installation.............KREUTZER......49
Hail to the Craft.........PARRY........43
From the North..........BASSFORD.....61
Anniversary Ode.........BERGE.........64

CHANTS, &c.

Entered Apprentice.....................70
Fellow Craft.............................72
Master Mason............................74
Gloria Tibi, No. 1......................70
Gloria Tibi, No. 2......................71
Gloria Tibi, No. 3......................72
Gloria Tibi, Ne. 4......................73

SWEET AS THE DEW

J. MOSENTHAL.

So with mild in-fluence from a - bove shall promised grace de -
So with mild in-fluence from a - bove shall promised grace de -
scend Till u - ni - ver - sal peace and love o'er all the earth ex - tend.
scend Till u - ni - ver - sal peace and love o'er all the earth ex - tend.

MEETING.

F. OTTO.

pp
With one ac - - cord Sweet as the
To swell their store So God doth
pp
With one ac - - cord Sweet as the
To swell their store So God doth
pp
fra - grance spread When o - ver Aa - rons head
shed his grace On ev - 'ry dwell - ing place
fra - grance spread When o - ver Aa - rons head
shed his grace On ev - 'ry dwell - ing place

The rich per - fume was shed That pleased the
Where love il - lumes the face Life ev er -
The rich per - fume was shed That pleased the
Where love il - lumes the face Life ev - er -
Lord That pleased the Lord.
- more Life ev - er - more.
Lord That pleased the Lord.
- more Life ev - er - more.

6735

BROTHERLY LOVE.

WORDS BY ARTHUR MATTHISON. KUCKEN.

o'er us the cy-press shall wave, shall wave Till o'er us the cypress shall
o'er us the cy-press shall wave, shall wave Till o'er us the cypress shall
wave........
Let love our watch-word be
wave........
Let love our watch-word be
SOLO
Let bro-ther-ly love our watch-word be, Let

pp
Let love our watch-word be While life shall last
pp
Let love our watch-word be While life shall last
pp
bro-ther-ly love our watch-word be
pp
cres. mf
sempre cres.
Till from earths sorrows free Make thy face on us to shine Grant
cres. mf
sempre cres.
Till from earths sorrows free Make thy face on us to shine Grant
mf
cres. mf
sempre cres.

ff
pp sempre piano e dol.
Lord thy grace di - vine Guide us O Lord un-till lifes scene shall close
ff
pp sempre piano e dol.
Lord thy grace di - vine Guide us O Lord un-till lifes scene shall close
ff
pp
sempre pi ano e dol.
ff
pp
poco ritard.
Grant us then Fa-ther e - ter-nal re - pose Grant e - ter-nal re - pose.
poco ritard.
Grant us then Fa-ther e - ter-nal re - pose Grant e - ter-nal re - pose.
poco ritard.

ETERNAL SOURCE. (L.M.)

FROM EAST TO WEST. (L.M.)

WITHIN OUR TEMPLE.

BRISTOW.

1. With-in our tem-ple met a - gain.... With hearts and
2. A-round our al-tar's sa-cred shrine... May loves pure

1 With-in our tem-ple met a - gain..... With hearts and
2. A-round our al-tar's sa-cred shrine.... May loves pure

pur - - - pose strong We'll raise our notes...........
in - - - cense rise Bear-ing up-on...........

We'll raise our
Bear-ing up-

pur - - - pose strong We'll raise our
in - - - cense rise Bear-ing up-

of
grate-ful praise
With
its
mys- tic flame
Our
notes...
on......
notes...
of grate-ful
praise
With
on.....
its mys - tic
flame
Our
u - nion in our song, With u - nion in our song.
mu - sic to the skies, Our mu - sic to the skies.
u - nion in our song, With u - nion in our song.
mu - sic to the skies, Our mu - sic to the skies.

FAR FROM THE WORLD'S.

REICHARDT.

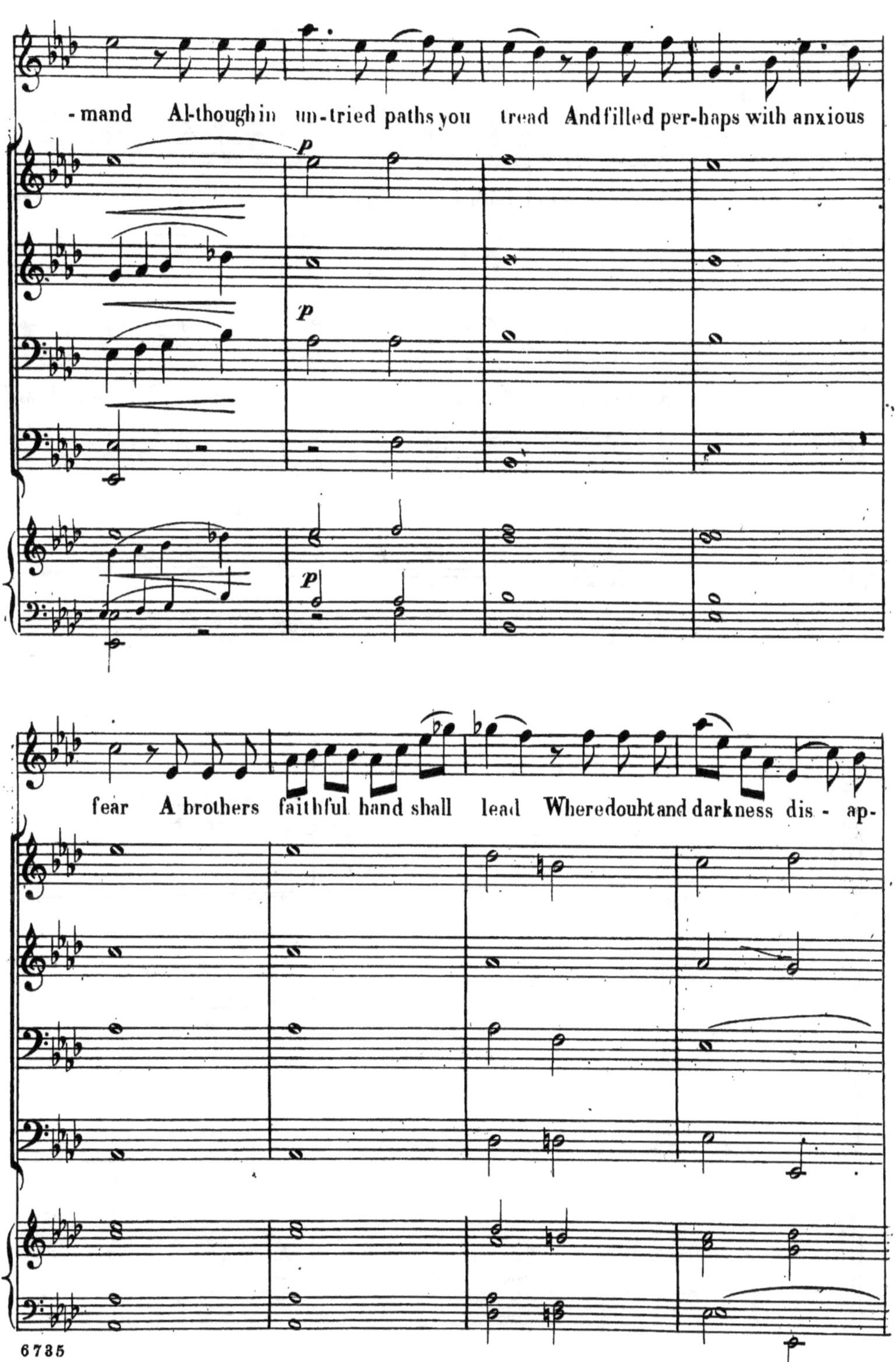
-mand Al-though in un-tried paths you tread And filled per-haps with anxious
p
p
p
fear A brothers faithful hand shall lead Where doubt and darkness dis - ap-

-pear.
Tutti. piu moto.
A bro-thers faith - ful hand shall lead.... Where doubt and
A bro-thers faith - ful hand shall lead.... Where doubt and
dark - ness dis - ap - pear Where doubt and dark - ness dis - ap - pear.
ten.
dark - ness dis - ap - pear Where doubt and dark - ness dis - ap - pear.

Solo. Molto espress.
CODA.
Tempo primo.
Where Truth and Love shall hold...... shall hold......
Where Truth and Love shall hold com - mand, hold.....
Where Truth and Love shall hold com - mand, hold......
.... com - mand, shall hold. com - mand....................
.... com - - mand, hold........ com - mand.
.... com - - - mand, hold........ com - mand.

SPIRIT OF POWER.

G. W. MORGAN.

ORGANIST M.W. GRAND LODGE STATE OF N.Y.

✻INTEGER VITAE.

FLEMMING.

✻May be sung when the Cantidate is in the N. E.

WELCOME.

J. R. THOMAS.

bow. Oh welcome if thy heart be true Thou'lt find with us a home;
now. Oh welcome if thy heart be true Thou'lt find with us a home;
bow. Oh wel - come if thy heart be true Thou'lt find with us a home;
now. Oh wel - come if thy heart be true Thou'lt find with us a home;
.... We're dai-ly ad-ding columns new, Un - to our glo-rious dome.
.... We're dai-ly ad-ding columns new, Un - to our glo-rious dome.
.... We're dai-ly ad-ding columns new, Un - to our glo-rious dome.
.... We're dai-ly ad-ding columns new, Un - to our glo-rious dome.

INITIATION.

HATTON.

pp
mf
path we tread When earth-ly ties shall fade and die When earth-ly joys shall
pp
mf
path we tread
When earth-ly joys shall
pp
mf
dim.
f
come no more
Thy Ho-ly aid when
dim.
p
f
come no more Su-preme con-duc-tor then supply Thy Ho-ly aid when
dim.
p
dim.
p
f

p dim.
time is o'er Thy
aid when time is
o'er....
p dim.
time is o'er Thy
aid when time is
o'er..................
p dim.
p dim.
Ho - ly
aid when
pp
time... is
o'er....
pp
Ho - ly
aid when
time... is
o'er....
pp
pp

INITIATION.

Dedicated to T. O. POLLOCK.

Wm BERGE. Mus. Doc.

now befriend Or
aid you in this
time of
need Con-
fide your trust in
now befriend Or
aid you in this
time of
need Con-
fide your trust in
him a-lone who
rules all things a-
bove, below.
Send your pe-ti-tions to his
him a-lone who
rules all things a-
bove, below.
Send your pe-ti-tions to his

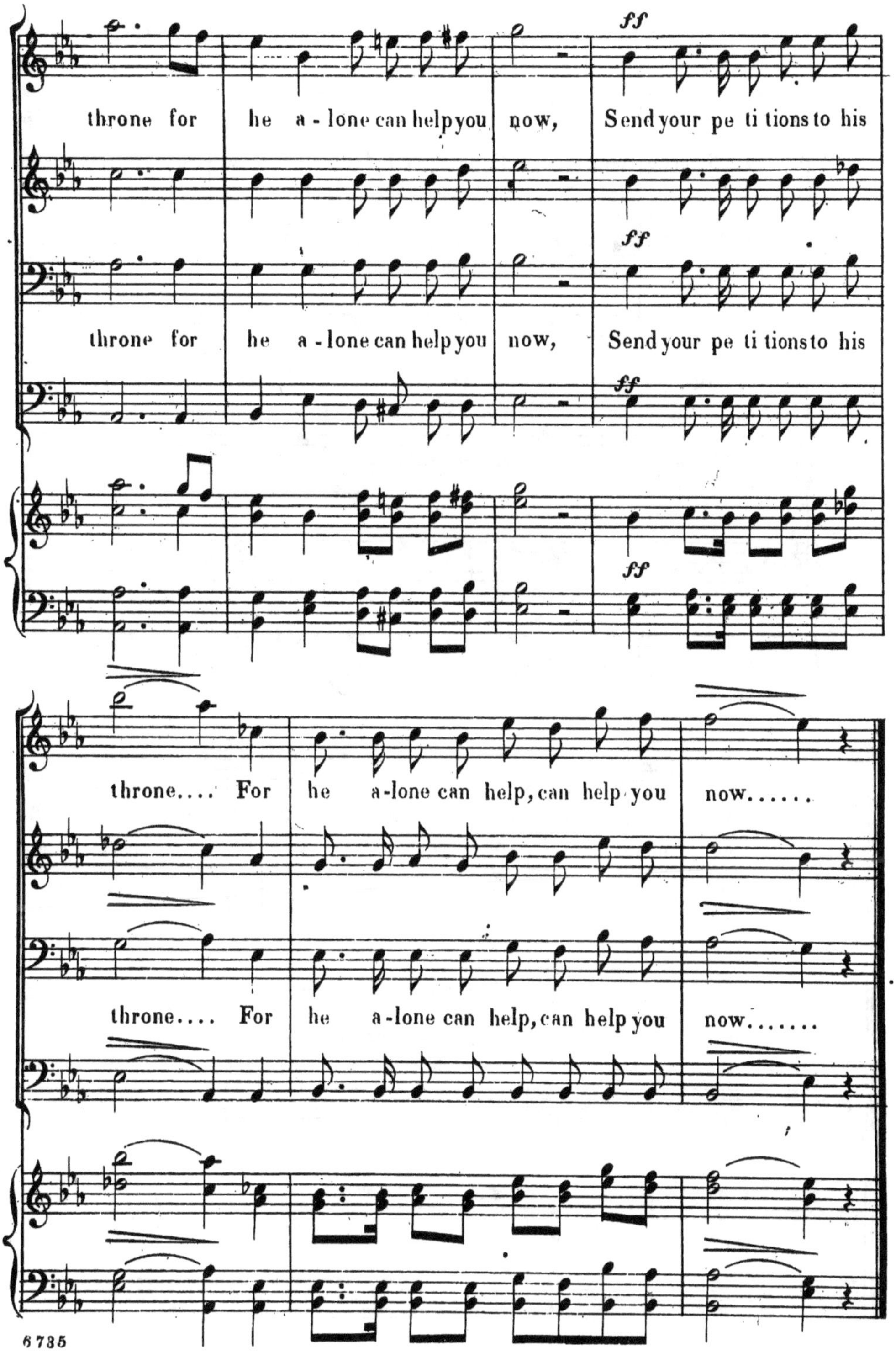

throne for he a - lone can help you now, Send your pe ti tions to his

throne for he a - lone can help you now, Send your pe ti tions to his

throne.... For he a-lone can help, can help you now......

throne.... For he a-lone can help, can help you now.......

QUARTETTO.

G. F. BRISTOW.

-veal their fear - ful pow-ers here. The vic - tor, death, and
save us in this try - ing hour. Oh! God of light, ex -
-veal their fear - ful pow-ers here. The vic - tor, death, and
save us in this try - ing hour. Oh! God of light, ex -
all things drear Re - veal their fear - ful pow - ers here.
-tend thy power, And save us in this try - ing hour.
all things drear Re - veal their fear - ful pow - ers here.
-tend thy power, And save us in this try - ing hour.

STRANGE DARKNESS.

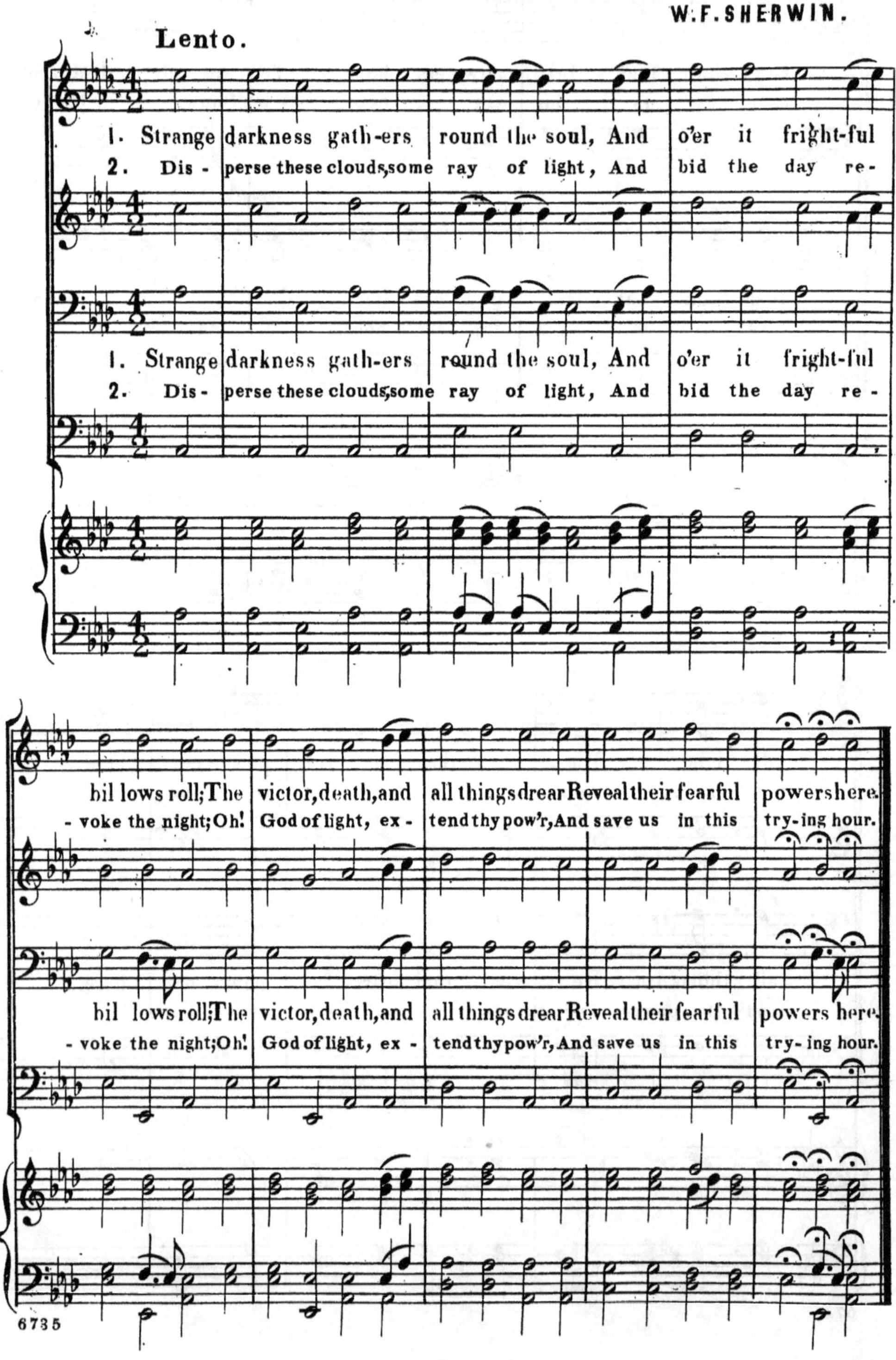

SWEET AS THE DEW.

C. A. MUNGER.

cres.
faithful hills On
Zi-ons
faithful
hills
So with mild
influence from a -
hills.....
cres.
faithful hills On
Zi-ons
faithful
hills
So with mild
influence from a -
cres.
cres.
- bove Shall
promised grace de-
scend, Shall
promised grace de-
scend Till
u-ni-versal
cres.
- bove Shall
promised grace de -
scend, Shall
promised grace de-
scend.
cres.

pp
peace and love, till
u- ni-versal
pp
mf
peace and love, O'er
all the earth ex
-tend,
pp
peace and
pp
pp
mf
pp
peace and love,
peace and love, O'er
all the earth ex
- tend,
peace and
pp
pp
mf
pp
pp
pp
mf
pp
mf
love O'er
all the earth ex-
tend
pp
peace and
f
love O'er
rit.
all the earth ex-
tend.
mf
pp
f
rit.
love O'er
all the earth ex-
tend
peace and
love O'er
all the earth ex-
tend.
mf
pp
f
rit.
mf
pp
f
rit.

LO! THE DAY AT LAST.

ARR FROM MARTHA.

p
Soft-ly now the dew is falling Peace o'er all the scene is spread On......his
p
Soft-ly now the dew is falling Peace o'er all the scene is spread On his
p
p
children, meekly call-ing purer influence God will shed. While thine ear of love ad -
pp
pp
children, meekly call-ing purer influence God will shed.
pp
sf
pp

-dress - ing,
Thus our part-ing
hymn we sing
Fa-ther give.... thy
parting bless -
ing
Fold us
safe
be-neath thy
wing.
p
pp
Father
Fold us safe.......
be-neath thy
wing.
p
pp
p
ppp

PARTING ODE.

O. A. MUNGER.

cres.
f
p
.... May love, re - lief and truth sin - cere U - nite each
cres.
f
p
May love, re - lief and truth sin - cere U - nite each
cres.
f
p
cres.
f
p
f
brothers heart. Now to our homes lets hast a - - way
f
lets haste a - way, lets haste a - way
brothers heart. Now to our homeslet haste a - way, lets haste a - way
f
lets hast a - - way
f

p
Still filled with love and light.... And may each heart in kind-ness
p
Still filled with love and light.... And may each heart in kind-ness
p
p
cres.
f
pp
ppp
say Good night brother good night.... Good night, Good night.
cres.
f
pp
ppp
say Good night brother good night.... Good night, Good night.
cres.
f
pp
ppp
cres.
f
pp
ppp

PARTING.

W. F. SHERWIN.

INSTALLATION.

G.W. MORGAN.
ORGANIST M.W. GRAND LODGE STATE OF N.Y.

serve him with free - dom fer - ver and zeal, And
aid him with free - dom fer - ver and zeal, And
aid him with free - dom fer - ver and zeal, And
serve him with free - dom fer - ver and zeal, And
aid him with free - dom fer - ver and zeal, And
aid him with free - dom fer - ver and zeal, And
aid him his du - ties and trust to ful - fil.
help him his du - ties and trust to ful - fil.
help him his du - ties and trust to ful - fil.
aid him his du - ties and trust to ful - fil.
help him his du - ties and trust to ful - fil.
help him his du - ties and trust to ful - fil.

HAIL TO THE CRAFT.

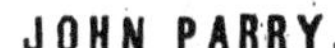

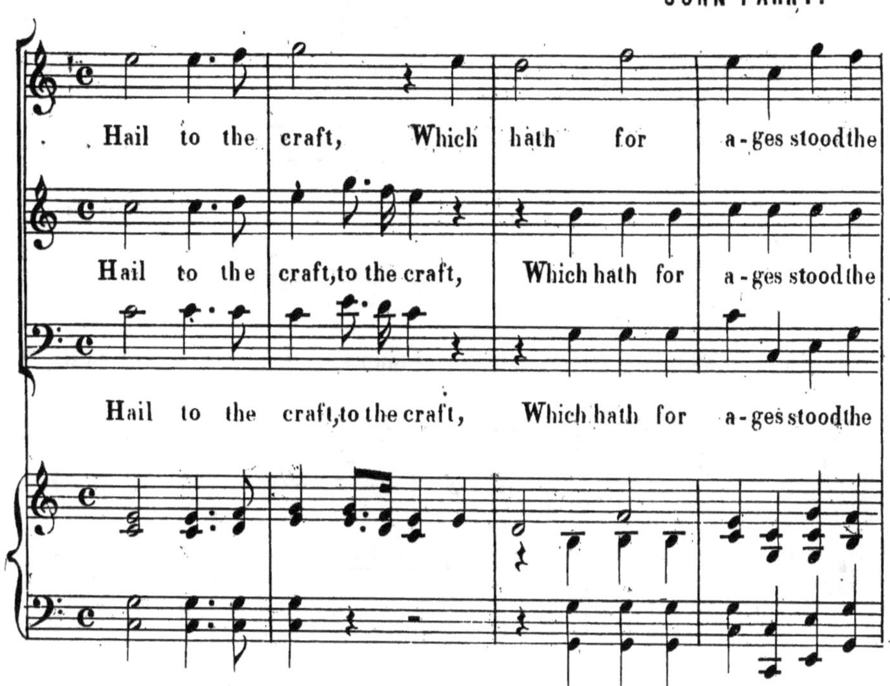

Which hath for a - ges stood the taunts of en - vy and the threats of
Which hath for a - ges stood the taunts of en-vy and
a - ges stood the taunts of en - vy and the threats of

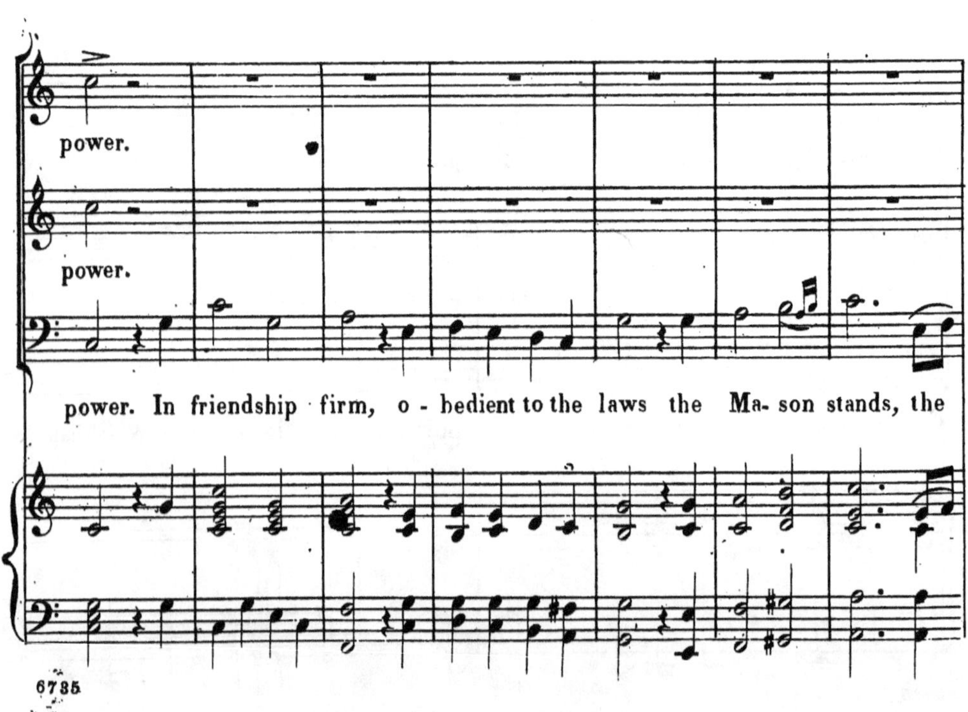
power.
power.
power. In friendship firm, o - bedient to the laws the Ma- son stands, the

In friendship firm o - bedient to the laws the
In friendship firm o - bedient to the laws
patriot and the man.
Ma - son stands,the patriot and the man. Hail to the craft, Which
the Ma-son stands,the patriot and the man. Hail to the craft,
Hail to the craft,Which hath for

hath for a - ges stood the taunts of en - vy and the threats of power.
Which hath for a - ges stood the taunts of en - vy and the threats of power.
a - ges stood the taunts of en - vy and the threats of power.
ad lib.
Fine.
Andante.
p
Hail to the craft, to the craft all hail.
When meek eyed pi-ty
ad lib.
p
Hail to the craft, to the craft all hail.
When meek eyed pi-ty
ad lib.
p
Hail to the craft, to the craft all hail.
When meek eyed pi-ty
Fine.
p

doth for aid im - plore... His heart ex - pands, she nev- er pleads in
doth for aid im - plore... His heart ex- pands, she nev- er pleads in
doth for aid im - plore... His heart ex- pands, she nev- er pleads in
vain...
vain.. The need - y's call... he free ly will o - - bey....
vain... And share the
6735

he'll share the gifts... that

he'll share the gifts... that

gifts..... that heav'n on him be - stows..........................

heav'n on him be - stows the giftsthat heav'nonhim be - stow..

heav'n on him be - stows he'll share the... giftsthat heav'nonhim be - stow..

the... giftsthat heav'nonhim be - stow..

D.C.

D.C.

INSTALLATION.

KREUTZER.

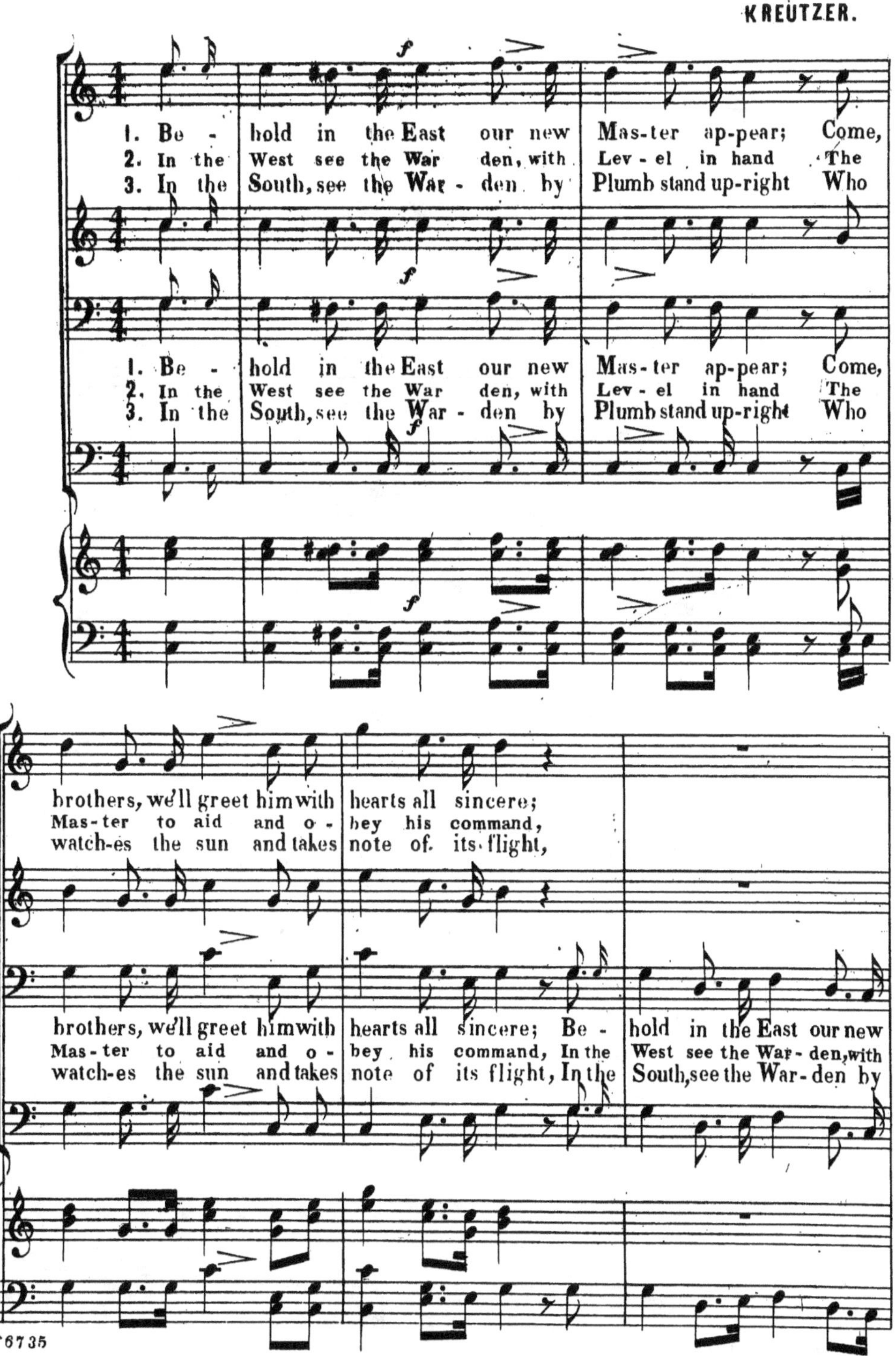

ff
pp
Come, brothers, we'll greet him with hearts all sincere; We'll
The Mas-ter to aid and o - bey his command We'll
Who watches the sun and takes note of its flight, We'll
ff
pp
Mas-ter ap-pear; Come, brothers we ll greet him with hearts all sincere; We'll
Lev - el in hand The Mas-ter to aid and o - bey his command We'll
Plumbstand upright Who watches the sun and takes note of its flight, We'll
ff
pp
pear
hand
right
ff
pp
serve him with freedom fer - vor and zeal, And aid him his du - ties and
aid him with free-dom fer - vor and zeal, And help him his du - ties and
aid him with freedom fer - vor and zeal, And help him his du - ties and
serve him with freedom fer - vor and zeal, And aid him his du - ties and
aid him with free-dom fer - vor and zeal, And help him his du - ties and
aid him with freedom fer - vor and zeal, And help him his du - ties and

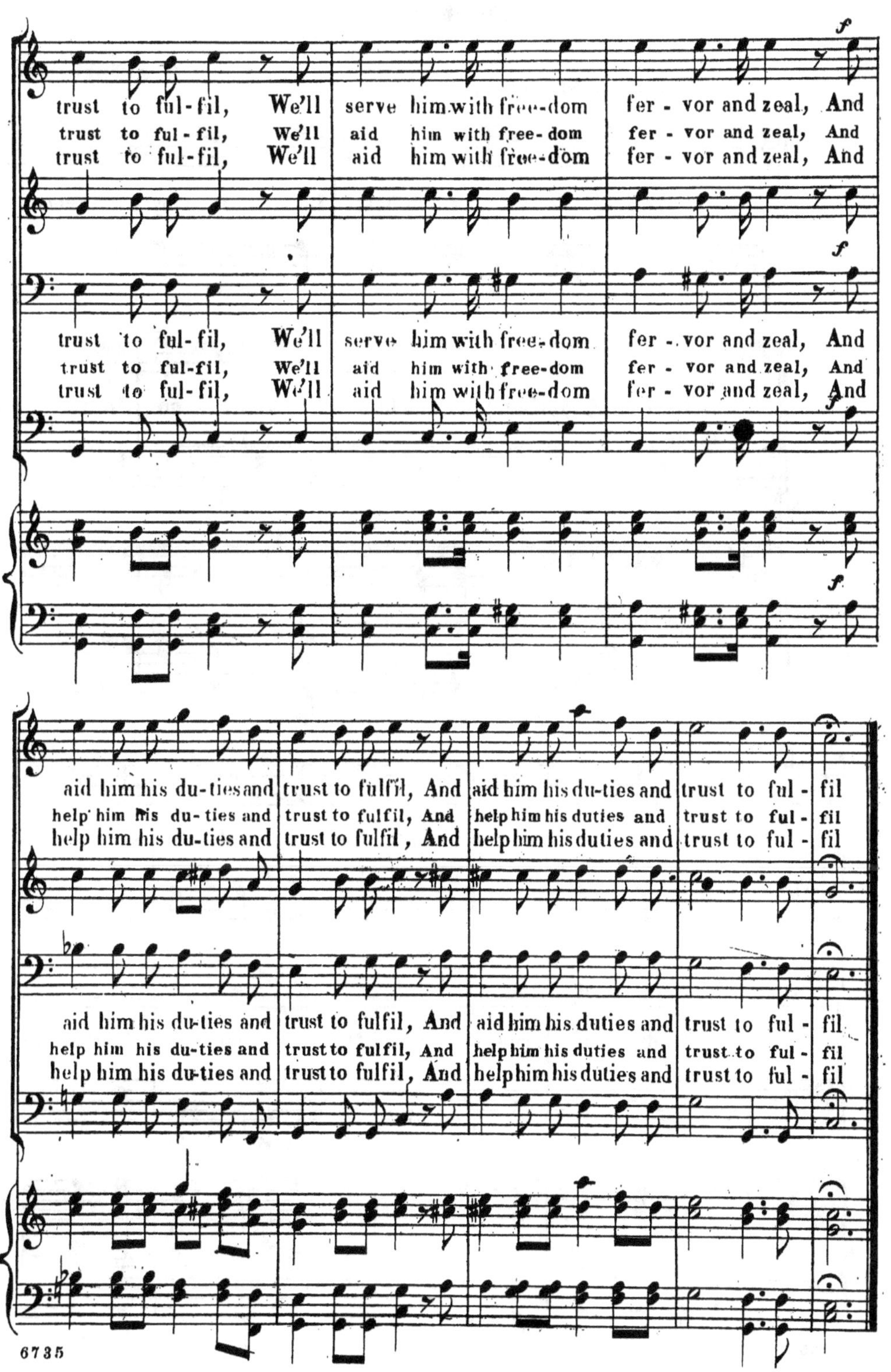
trust to ful-fil, We'll serve him with free-dom fer - vor and zeal, And
trust to ful-fil, We'll aid him with free-dom fer - vor and zeal, And
trust to ful-fil, We'll aid him with free-dom fer - vor and zeal, And
trust to ful-fil, We'll serve him with free-dom fer - vor and zeal, And
trust to ful-fil, We'll aid him with free-dom fer - vor and zeal, And
trust to ful-fil, We'll aid him with free-dom fer - vor and zeal, And
aid him his du-ties and trust to fulfil, And aid him his du-ties and trust to ful - fil
help him his du-ties and trust to fulfil, And help him his duties and trust to ful - fil
help him his du-ties and trust to fulfil, And help him his duties and trust to ful - fil
aid him his du-ties and trust to fulfil, And aid him his duties and trust to ful - fil
help him his du-ties and trust to fulfil, And help him his duties and trust to ful - fil
help him his du-ties and trust to fulfil, And help him his duties and trust to ful - fil

HEAR MY PRAYER.

W. K. BASSFORD.

Hide not then, Thy gra - cious face, When the storm a - round me falls,
Hide not then, Thy gra - cious face, When the storm a - round me falls,
PP Play right hand an octave lower.
Hear Thy servant God of grace When on Thee he hum - bly calls.
Hear Thy servant God of grace When on Thee he hum - bly calls.
poco rall
6735

THE LAST DEGREE.

rall.
sha - - - dows of the tomb? Up-ward still! on God re-
morn - - ings gold - en ray. Nev - er doubt - ing nev - er
rall.
sha - - - dows of the tomb? Up-ward still! on God re-
morn - - ings gold - en ray. Nev - er doubt - ing nev - er
rall.
- ly - ing; Lo! the clouds are fa-ding now; Hear the
fear - ing, God our hope while time doth run; Clear-er
- ly - ing; Lo! the clouds are fa-ding now; Hear the
fear - ing, God our hope while time doth run; Clear-er

voice of Hope re - ply- ing While in trust we humbly bow, Hear the
still, our way ap - pear-ing, Till the Last De-gree be won! Clearer
voice of Hope re - ply-ing While in trust we humbly bow, Hear the
still, our way ap - pear-ing, Till the Last De-gree be won! Clearer
f
rall.
voice of Hope re - ply - ing While in trust we hum - bly bow.
still, our way ap - pear - ing, Till the Last De - gree be won!
voice of Hope re - ply - ing While in trust we hum - bly bow.
still, our way ap - pear - ing, Till the Last De - gree be won!
6735

WHILE JOURNEYING ON.

HENRY C. WATSON.

p
dolce.
assia.
fear shall cross the trusting heart, Our faith re-pos'd in Him a-bove; No fear shall
p
dolce.
assia.
fear shall cross the trusting heart, Our faith re-pos'd in Him a-bove; No fear shall
p
dolce.
assia.
cross the trusting heart, Our faith re-pos'd on Him a-bove; No dear-er
pp
pp
cross the trusting heart, Our faith re-pos'd on Him a-bove; No dear-er
pp
pp

dolce.
ff
pp
joy can life im- part, Than gent-ly breathes in words of love, gent- ly
dolce.
ff
pp
joy can life im- part, Than gent-ly breathes in words of love,
ff
ff
pp
p
rall
a tempo.
pp
breathes in words of love, gently breathes in words of... love.. When earthly ties shall
dolce.
p
p
rall
pp
a tempo.
breathes in words of love, breathes in words of... love.. When earthly ties shall
dolce.
p
a tempo.
p
p
rall
pp

p
cres.
ff
fade and die, When earthly joys shall come no more Su-preme Crea-tor! then supply
p
cres.
ff
fade and die, When earthly joys shall come no more Su-preme Crea-tor! then supply
p
p
cres.
ff
Thy holy aid, when time is o'er, Thy ho-ly aid, when time is o'er...
Thy holy aid, when time is o'er, Thy ho-ly aid, when time is o'er...

FROM THE NORTH.

West in each land neath the sun Our proud tem-ples a - dorn the wide
tar-nished and pure shall they be Till the world from cre - a - tion shall
West in each land neath the sun Our proud tem-ples a - dorn the wide
tar-nished and pure shall they be Till the world from cre - a - tion shall
world Fra - ter - nal- ly bonded con - cor - dant- ly joined Our
pass When of old the wise Po-ten. - tate found-ed our Craft From e-
world Fra - ter - nal - ly bonded con - cor- dant- ly joined Our
pass When of old the wise Po-ten - tate found-ed our Craft From e-

hands meet in brother-ly clasp And when palm clings to palm knit by
- ter - ni - tys rock sprang the tree Let us swear love to man, un-to
hands meet in brother-ly clasp And when palm clings to palm knit by
- ter - ni - tys rock sprang the tree Let us swear love to man, un-to
mys - ti - cal sign Our souls vi-brates deep with the grasp.
God faith and truth Till e - ter - ni - ty, Broth - ers we see.
mys - ti - cal sign Our souls vi-brates deep with the grasp.
God faith and truth Till e - ter - ni - ty, Broth - ers we see.

ANNIVERSARY ODE.

Wm BERGE. Mus. Doc.

Se - ra-phim
Join'd in one
Glo-rious hymn
Be-fore the
throne.
Se - ra-phim
Join'd in one
Glo-rious hymn
Be-fore the
throne.
Maestoso e Grandioso.
mf
cres.
ff
God their Grand Master
was
Fixed their unerring
laws
By his de
- cree
God their Grand Master
was
Fixed their unerring
laws
By his de
- cree
Maestoso e Grandioso.

ff
Faith, Hope, and
Cha-ri-ty,
Friendship and
U - ni - ty
Truth, Love and
ff
Faith, Hope, and
Cha-ri-ty,
Friendship and
U - ni - ty
Truth, Love and
ff
ff
p
Se - cre - cy
All laws di -
vine.
Oh may our
constant theme To
p
Se - cre - cy
All laws di -
vine.
Oh may our
constant theme To
p
p

Heavns Great King Su - preme Be grateful Love; Be grate-ful Love;
Heavns Great King Su - preme Be grateful Love; Be grate-ful Love;
Con moto.
May we when e'er we meet Chant Hal-le-lu-jahs sweet,
May we when e'er we meet Chant Hal-le-lu-jahs sweet,
Con moto.

And three times three re - peat Je - ho - vahs praise May we when e'er we
And three times three re - peat Je - ho - vahs praise May we when e'er we
Piu mosso.
meet Chant Halle-lu - jahs sweet And three times three re - peat Je -
meet Chant Halle-lu - jahs sweet And three times three re - peat Je -
Piu mosso.

presto.
-ho - vahs
praise
May we whene'er we
meet
Chant Hal-le-lu - jahs
presto.
-ho - vahs
praise
May we whene'er we
meet
Chant Hal-le-lu - jahs
presto.
sweet
And three times three re -
peat Je -
- ho -
vahs
praise.
sweet
And three times three re -
peat Je -
- ho -
vahs
praise.

ENTERED APPRENTICE.

C. A. MUNGER.

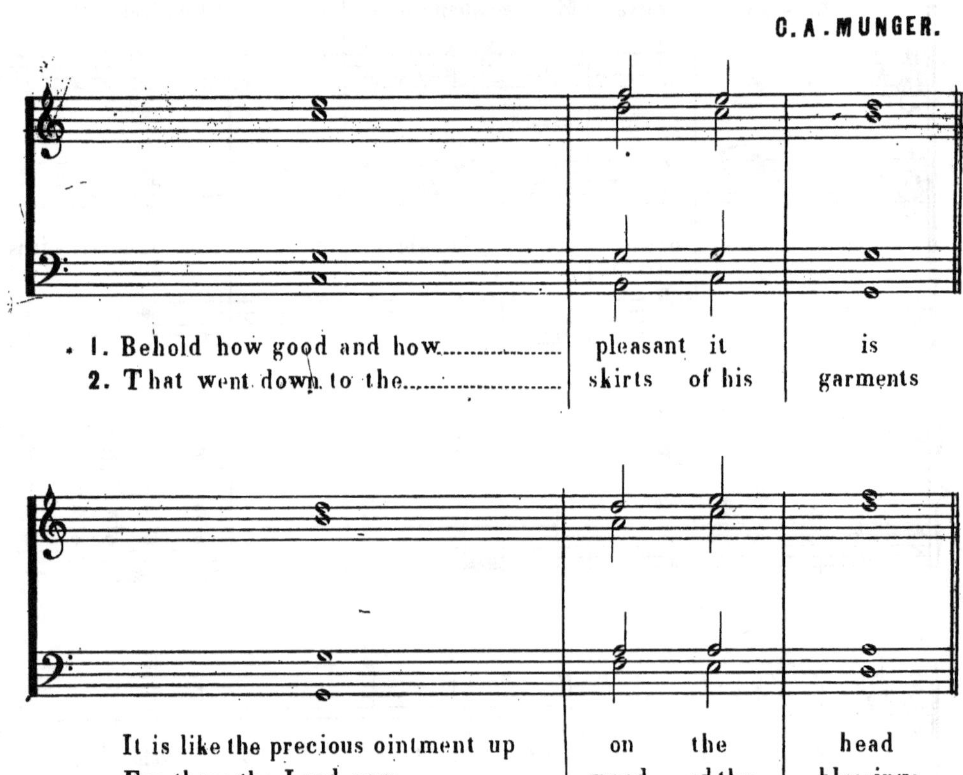

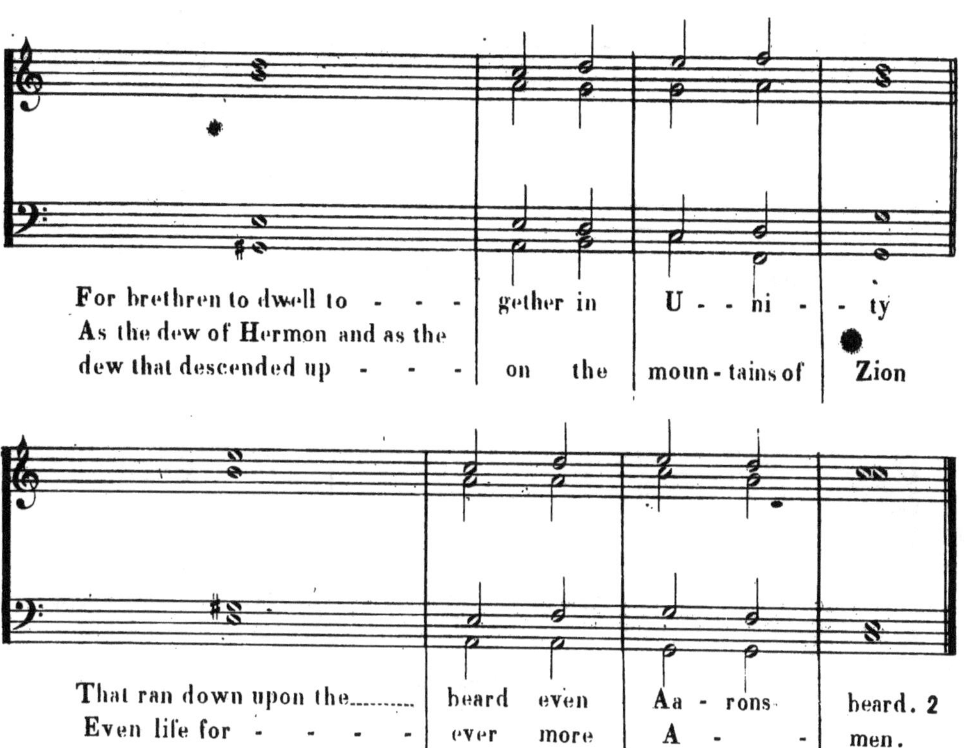

GLORIA TIBI. No II.

BERGE.

FELLOW CRAFT.

C. A. MUNGER.

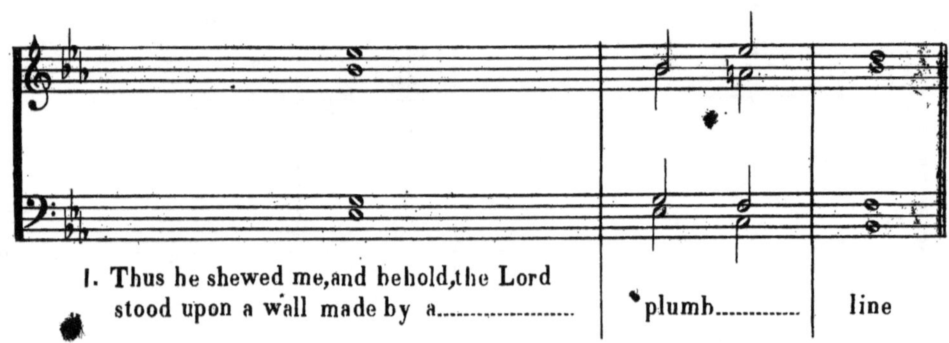

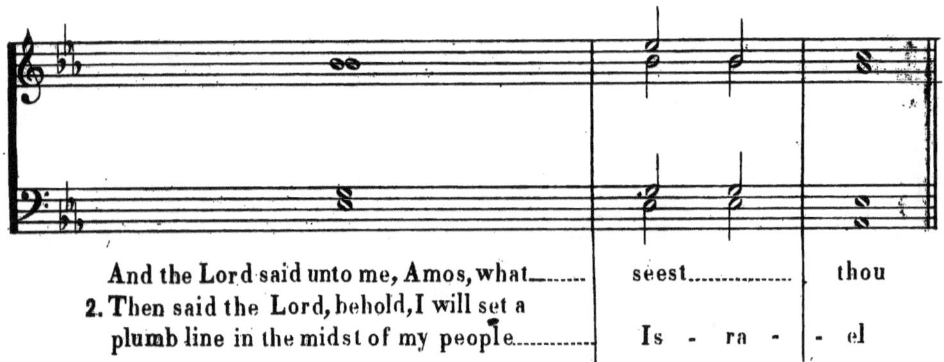

GLORIA TIBI No III.

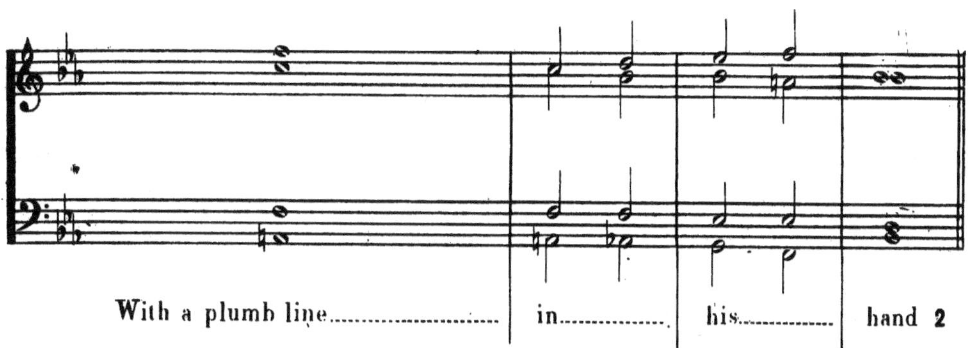

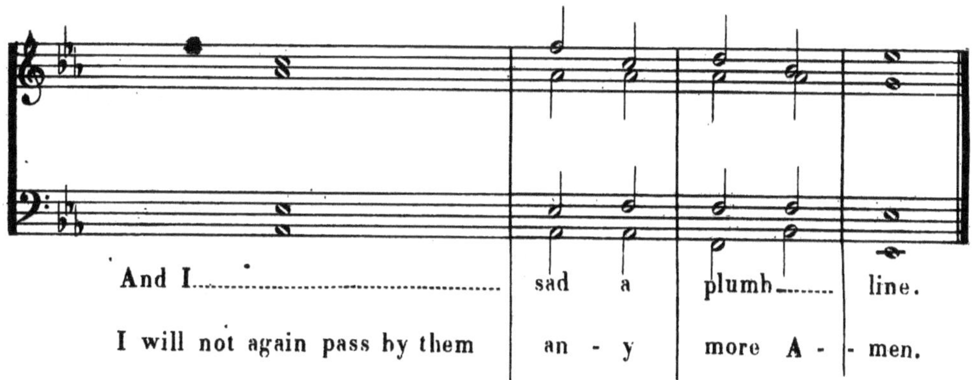

GLORIA TIBI. Nº IV.

G.W. MORGAN.

MASTER MASON.

C.A.MUNGER.

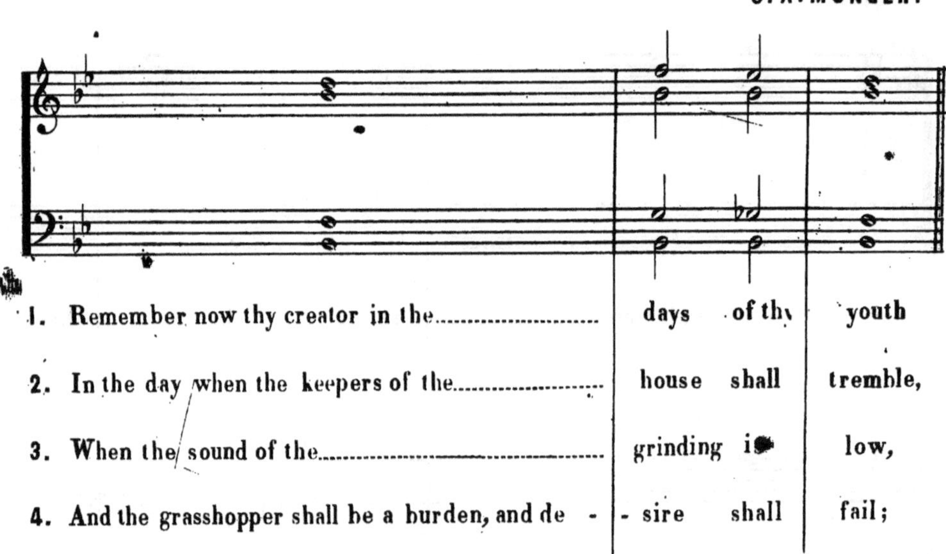

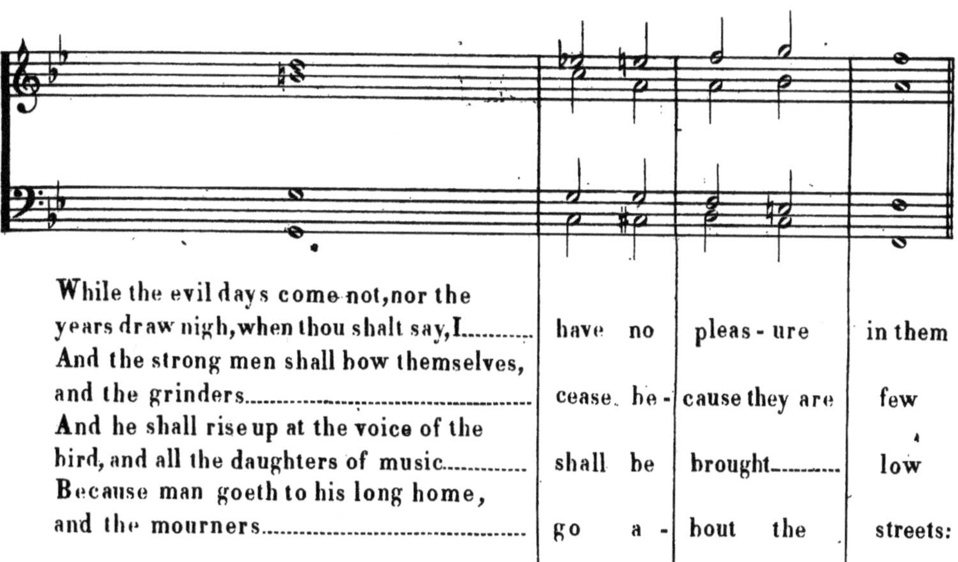
While the evil days come not, nor the years draw nigh, when thou shalt say, I | have no | pleas - ure | in them
And the strong men shall bow themselves, and the grinders | cease, be - | cause they are | few
And he shall rise up at the voice of the bird, and all the daughters of music | shall be | brought | low
Because man goeth to his long home, and the mourners | go a - | bout the | streets:

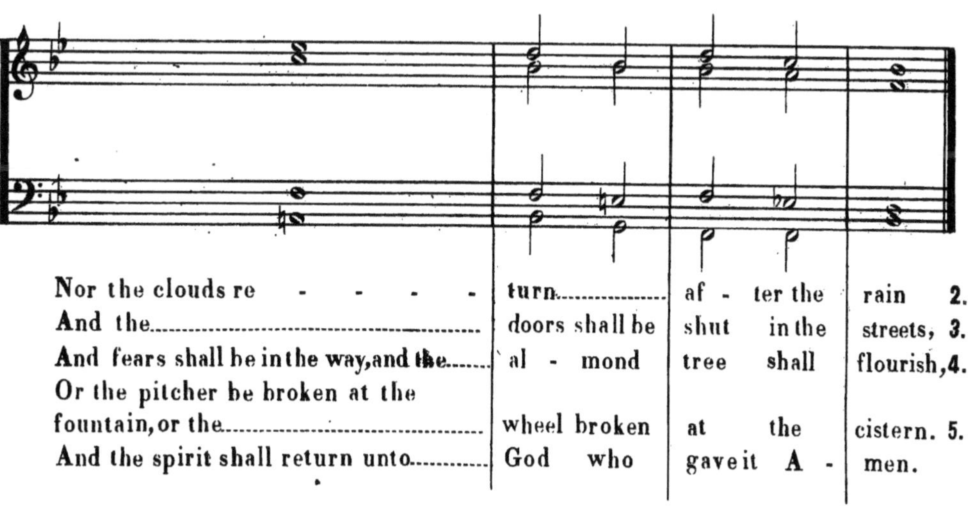
Nor the clouds re - - - - | turn | af - ter the | rain 2.
And the | doors shall be | shut in the | streets, 3.
And fears shall be in the way, and the | al - mond | tree shall | flourish, 4.
Or the pitcher be broken at the fountain, or the | wheel broken | at the | cistern. 5.
And the spirit shall return unto | God who | gave it A - | men.

www.ingramcontent.com/pod-product-compliance
Lightning Source LLC
Chambersburg PA
CBHW051228290326
41931CB00042B/3425
9781935907466